The Open Mind

Loving Your Self

Thank You
Laura
for Being in my life
as we walk Home
Together

914
969-3393   Love
          DAVID

The Open Mind

Loving Your Self

David Fishman

Edited by
Valinda Vujovich

One Spirit Press
onespiritpress.com
Portland, Oregon

It
does start
within
Your Mind

Thoughts and Prayers
Along the Way

Foreword

There is no new knowledge. No special wisdom that awaits our discovery. We step into this world complete and All-Knowing Beings. Our task is simply one of remembering.

Layer by layer, we peel away the perceptual falsehoods we've wrapped ourselves in the name of safety. We are really here... trying to remember we are the Love and the Light, called into the duality of this world.

Every moment a step closer to Home and the oneness our hearts remember. To be a journey of joy and adventure, we often forget and wander lost into the illusion. It is from this place, that your heart calls to Love, "What have I forgotten?". Love gently answers, "your Truth is within you, and you are safe and youare loved."

The Open Mind , answers that call to Love. A gentle reminder that , "All is Well" and a bright light on your journey into Peace and into oneness.

In full appreciation of this journey we walk together, We share these moments of oneness with You.

In Peace and in Love,

Let us ask
for The **Peace of God**
which is ours to shine forth and let us
join with our brothers
everywhere
as ONE
Amen

PREFACE

Committed to the idea that we are truly *one* and our only purpose here is to remember this fact, and return to our timeless oneness, which we have always shared with God, Our Father and Creator in reality, is the inspiration and premise of *Into Oneness*.

Given our human condition of forgetting our true identity, the mind/body that serves us, sees and hears what it needs to survive in a world that appears to support our belief in separation from each other and from God.

This mindset which we are born into and believe in, sees this physical world as *this is all there is*. Our mind's conditioning keeps this misperception as *sacred* unless we are given an alternate choice, and choose once again, what is real and what we have made to *appear real*.

In contrast to this conflicted mind process the ideas and thoughts presented herein are sourced from *A Course of Miracles,* originally published in 1975 by *The Foundation of Inner Peace*, now located in Temeculah, CA.

Its message is a re-mind-er that we are all connected to a Divine Source which we can choose to listen to that has a radically different way of seeing the people and world we line in. This source knows our best interest for It knows us.

If we choose to develop and use these thoughts as our own, we begin our Awakening from the deep sleep of forgetfulness. Peace of Mind is our primary goal on this *path home as we walk together into oneness.*

With peace, comes a transformation from our conflicted values to clarity and lightness, which reveals *our true shining self* that lights the way for others. Laughter, in the face of the grim realties of this world is a sure sign that we have seen past the illusions to what is *real.*

The Great Awakening, which is our step into oneness, is our awareness of the humor that this Cosmic Joke, which we have played on our Self, is merely *a dream of separation, without any real effects.*

Our task is to understand what we made is unreal.

We walk together... always remembering that each one we meet along the way is truly us, if we choose to see their true beauty and perfection. Each of us serves as a living lesson for another. When acknowledged and learned correctly, we are free of our self-imposed belief in the limitations of the body and the conflicting dramas played out in this world's events.

In full appreciation
for your participation in this journey
We take together,

David Fishman

Yes.
We are ONE
ONE Father
ONE Home
ONE Mind
ONE Son
and that is what we celebrate.
every day.
And every week.
Until that which is real
is what we know

...and nothing else.

ACIM Teaches...A Curriculum...
which is the exact opposite of the world's curriculum.
So that is why I say
that I would love to Teach
that part of my Self
the principles of the Course
as if I were to start from scratch.

First...
We made this world.
This is what we made
as an attack upon love,
our self, and our Creator
in an attempt to forget our *true identity.*
We are powerful...creators.
We made a world
that serves to keep us asleep.
We have made an illusionary world
and have taken on our mind/body suits
and entered a world
that is totally opposite to our home.
We are blessed
and I am grateful
as I know you All are
that ACIM has come into our Life...
this dreamlike state
to say...WAKE UP!

What you are looking at
and what you are thinking
is what you made up
as a way to avoid

and filter out and not see
your self.

The first 2 lessons
of the course tell you this.
Lesson 1 says
what I see is meaningless
and lesson 2 says
that whatever meaning I see
I have made it up and see exactly
what I want to see.

If we just dwell on these first 2 lessons
we would begin to understand
what we have gotten ourselves into.

Of course lessons 3 and 4
go right into the same thought
about the thoughts in our mind
saying that they are meaningless
and we have given each of the thoughts
the meaning they have for us.

So we see a pattern here.
We have made a world
which has no meaning
except for the meaning
which we gave to it
and that is to stay
locked into our dream-like
illusions.

The Course comes into ours lives
And asks for Saviors.
And here a Savior is One
who first Heals or AWAKENS
and then can Help
in the Healing and Extending of Love
to His Brothers
who temporarily are still
in the dream and asleep.

Practicing the Course literally means
remembering this
and spending time
for that is the purpose of time
to begin to let go
of the dreamlike stuff
which we have accumulated along the way
and Be With Our Father
Who Art in Heaven...With US.

These moments...minutes...and hours
spent in this way
is practicing the Course.
The rest comes easy.
For once we have an Idea
of Who We are
Healing our relationships
with our Brother comes naturally.
What we find ourselves stuck in...
is the meaningless stuff we have made up.
in a world that was purposely made...to deceive us.
as to who we are...

who Our Brother IS
and our Connection to Him

 Who is ONE with US...

None of this is obvious
or clear in this world
for the world was made
to mask the Truth from us
a veil or curtain drawn
over our Self...
and it is so easy...
to forget this
ONENESS
in this world...
until we take time out...for practicing ...
returning to this
ONENESS.

And I believe
that this is what
ACIM
has come to say
and it is what I would
Teach to my Self

if I was going to start from scratch.

Good Morning Sonshine!

...after I realize
that I am descending down the steps...
I do say...whatever IT is...
I am making something
that is valueless
very Valuable
or...I am making something
based on separation and judgment
very real.

These are the same.
Usually...it is enough
to let me begin
to get Bigger then the "littleness"
that I am looking at...
and Ask for Peace

as Soon

as Possible.

When we and the Holy Spirit
Asking is giving
and the **only** thing we can give
is seeing our brother as
one with us
as *The Son of God*.
For this is
All that the
Holy Spirit
recognizes.

Everything
is
for your own
best interest
...including this moment.

YOU ARE THE SON OF GOD.
Yet, we cannot know our Self
until we are willing to See our Brother
as The Son of God.
Anything else that we use
as a distraction from that Vision,
keeps Us from fulfilling our Only Function here.
So...no matter what your Brother says
or does...
INCLUDE HIM...as YOU,
THE SON OF GOD.
Only that is worth...the term...
Healing.

That is the Choice...
to See Him Truly.
Not as we saw him in the past,
but to see Him as He IS NOW,
and ALWAYS...as YOU!
I know this is not always easy
yet every time we can do this
for to choose this,
is the speeding up of our Own Healing.

And is this not worth it?
Many times in the Text
it speaks of Forgiveness
as a Selfish process
and by this it does mean...
that we do this...
for Our Self...
for in Our Brother's Freedom,
from what we would make of him,
Is our Own release
and Freedom too
from the
laws of chaos.

Let us
Remember
our True Self
One that is
Our Center
One that Is
Peaceful
When only we remember
Only Perfect Love exists and
We Are
as Love Created US.

What we are Asking for...
is to be UNITED
with the Sonship,
the WHOLENESS,
the ONE Creation.
When we Look on our Brother
we can either see his body...
or See His Holiness.
The choice is always ours.
And the results is also ours.
If we choose to see His Holiness,
His Oneness with US...
To Be Joined In The Christ within Him...or Her...
It is the Christ...which is the Light within us...
that we Hear.
It says in the Course...
when we Ask to see His Holiness
that is a sign from us
that we want the Holy Spirit to Guide US.
You have taken the first step...
a very necessary step,
in the unlearning process

The Course tells us in so many ways
that the NOW...is the ONLY place
we can KNOW...Our Self.
Lesson 7 says...
"We see only the past".
So given this background,
which is the ego's backyard,
it takes a WHOLE lot of Vigilance
to BE HERE NOW!
It is in the Stillness...the Quiet of
NOW...
that The Peace of God...doesn't come.
IT IS ALREADY HERE WITH US...
it IS OURS NOW!
Of course...our limited idea of Now
is that it lasts but a moment.
Yet, in the Quiet Mind...the Now...
is Eternal.
Lesson 182, says...
"I will be still an instant and go home".
It says this...since...HOME is Eternal
and in Fact we are at HOME
ALWAYS.

Even if our minds have this
fascination with the past,
or said in other words,
an investment in dreams,
a big investment that is,
Only by being still...
an instant
can we
Know the Peace...of God.
Which is requisite
to enter the Kingdom...
Home
Nothing...outside of us
can possibly offer
what we
Truly want and HAVE.
For as the Course says...
Being and Having
are ONE and the Same
and the only way we can
BE...Our Self
Is in the Now.

Even though...we do think
we can correct our Brother,
we can't.
In a way...it is just like judgment.
Yet...when we judge...
we all know that we are judging
and then we catch ourselves...and Voila!!!
We say...OOPS...there I go again!
Listening to the ego.
OOPS!!!...Wrong teacher!
Now...in correcting our Brother...
it appears much more subtle.
YET...it is the same.
Yet...it is much more insidious.
Since...when we do it...
it is "me the nice guy"
helping my Brother...find his way.
YET...we are listening to the ego.
For only the ego...sees the need to correct.
For only the ego...sees error.
Thus...we come up with
"IYSIYGI..." • If You Spot It...You Got It...

We all make mistakes...
and have goofed,
and listened to the ego.
But...on another level,
we are speaking from the identity
that sees itself
...as less...not whole.
And we are speaking
from our wrong-mindedness.
THUS...
Healing is not possible.
And since HEALING
is the Purpose of ACIM,
Understanding the dynamics
of Correction
IS HEALING...TO OUR SELF!

I watched my mind
see him as "not the same as me."
At least in his understanding
of what I understood.
Now...THAT IS THE EGO...
setting someone, my Brother,
apart from me...a judgment
that I not only CANNOT make
but a distraction from my
Purpose for being here,
For Healing...the Joining with My Brother...
and the Recognition that we are ONE.
Which is the Truth.
Anything less than this
is more of the ego's teachings...
which I can follow...yet...I need to know
that this is not Healing.
It is just more of the same...
that I came to undo.

Remember the Venus de Milo story...
Why does Venus, the symbol of Love,
have no arms?
Because...
Love doesn't have to reach out...
EVERYTHING
comes to LOVE.

The stars need no words...
yet they shine brilliantly forever
sometimes...
words really get in the way
...as you know

ASK...what is this FOR?
Is it for MY purpose?
Once you can say Yes...
to this question,
whatever you are "thinking" about
becomes something
you need not pursue.
Unless you feel you still want whatever.
So in this you have free will.
...if you can say...
THE PURPOSE is FOR...
THE HEALING of the SONSHIP
and NOT your own use...
you need not think about it
anymore.
...FOR IT SHALL BE DONE.

We Ask The Holy Spirit...
That We Awaken
to Our True Identity
and See The Son of God
In Everyone We meet
Amen

When we hold on...we retain,
and retaining...keeps the mind busy.
The mind works on whatever we hold on to.
Btw...that is how Einstein came to
his understandings
of the physical universe...
by having his mind work on it!!
Yes! That cute thing we made...
to occupy time and space...
which we made to have the mind
keep us busy.
Kind of like a 4-dimensional crossword puzzle.
It gives you clues...
you figure it out...
and fill in the spaces.
Of course...the more spaces we fill in...
the more spaces we still have to fill in...
it's a perpetual motion machine
designed to keep us...
ASLEEP!!!
There is never an end to time and space
until we are ready...
TO WAKE UP.
To AWAKEN from the dream...
That there is something else.

Just part of the virtual reality machine.
Lessons in all of it.
Not to fret.
Just to walk smoothly thru
and keep your head up high.
Don't be afraid
of the dark...
I feel a song coming on..

There is nothing to wait for.
Nothing to have to do.
You don't have to finish anything.
YOU ARE CAUSE...
and THE SOURCE is with YOU>>>NOW!!
Not later.
The thought I am not ready...
is the worlds whole thought system.
It is another way...of saying...
I am NOT WHOLE...or Complete.
One day...I will be.
But not now.
Fear is always the block
to the Thought of
Perfection and Wholeness.
The fear is what prevents us...NOW.
IF GOD IS WITH YOU...
Who could be against you?????
Only our judgments,
which are always of the ego.
And since the ego...itself...is nothing...
but an idea that we made up...
so are its judgments.
Which will fade into the nothingness
from which they are made

SHARE
YOUR
AWESOMENESS!!!

The answer you are looking for
is within you...
There is a very powerful being within
who is invulnerable
to the nightmares of the dream.
And this is what
you must get in touch with.
Vigilance
of the mind
is about bringing yourself...
to the NOW.
We can't find ourselves in the past...
or in the future,
only in the Now.
When you find your strength...
your Mind...
will bring a
Peaceful outcome.

.

Insanity is not easy to understand...
unless
you too
are insane...

Anything less than letting go
amounts to a grievance...
and only our grievances
can hurt us.
So we either SHINE
or we are bottled up...
with our grievances
blotting out our Light.

Focus on the Light
and IT WILL EXPAND
and EXTEND.

Get out of the way...
and let it happen
the only one you are blocking
...is your SELF.
You know ...
when you are hanging onto something
and you have to protect it,
you are "filled" with...
protecting.
When you give it all up...
You can laugh...at it all...

The People I have met
through my life,
all of them,
were each
Blessings.
Some of them,
I recognized immediately.
Some later.
And some I thought
I would not ever see
as Blessings.
Yet as time went by
and the Light Came ON
I began to see each and EVERY person
as A BLESSING.
Which is what the Course tells us
IS TRUE.
For they are US.
The ones who did not appear
to be at first,
were probably
our greatest
Blessings.

Then Let us REMEMBER THIS NITE...
WHEN WE COUNTED OUR BLESSINGS...
and TAKE THEM WITH US...
where we go...
and LET OUR LIGHT AND BLESSINGS SHINE...
as IT INCREASES IN MAGNITUDE
GOD BLESSES...
and WE EXTEND
THANK YOU!!
Amen

Tonite we Gather Together...
To Give Thanks and Gratitude...
for having Chosen ACIM...
and to Give Jesus
Our Thanks
for Sharing it with US...
ALL
here and now...
for the world would look
a lot different...to us...
without A Course in Miracles...
so for ALL that we have Received
and Given...
we say...
Amen

The Course
and its Purpose...
has become my Own.
And for that I am very Glad
that Purpose and Function...
is Healing...
to Heal MySelf!
Its Goal...
which is Peace...
Peace of Mind...
Is my Goal.
And I like to say
Peace NOW.
For this is the only time there is.

I see God, My Father...
as I see myself...in many ways.
As Loving.
And could not imagine...anything else.
I have found myself
Sharing...
and Accepting...
what I could not have ever accepted
in an earlier time of my life.
I do believe...that the Course
does do that for all of us.
In giving us an understanding
that this world...which we made...
is exactly that.
Something we made...and nothing else.
And as Students and Teachers of the Course,
we are given a new Curriculum...
To Teach Our Self.
And I am never fooled by the fact, that,
I am really Teaching my Self...
that which I most need to learn

The idea that we only Teach our SELF...
has a similar idea in the Course.
And this is what I feel
I have possibly gained the most
from my Study of the Course,
And that is the idea...
that we are
ONE.
And if I see a brother as having erred
and needs correction...
Then it is I...
who still needs the correction.

Let US come
with Open Hearts
and Empty Minds
to ASK
For HIS PEACE
so we may Be Filled
With His Understanding
and For this
We Give
OUR THANKS and Gratitude
Amen

As long as we choose
to hear the Teaching of the ego...
we cannot hear the Teacher of Peace.
For we are filled with the teaching of this world.
And this world is made
to deceive us as to who we are.
It is a distraction.
And as long as we listen to the distractions
and think we know...
WHO WE ARE...WE DON'T
for their very intention...
and meaning...
is to obscure that from us.
That is why the Course...asks us to come with
Empty Hands...
Open Minds...
and to
HAVE PEACE..
as our ONLY GOAL..
or anything else
will be the ego's goal...
who knows not what we want.
It is not its function...
so it is clueless.

I always love
how Lesson 1 and 2
and 3 and 4
pretty much
tell us the same thing...
We made it all up.
And until we accept this...
the beat goes on.

Dear Father
WE GIVE THANKS...
for YOUR PEACE...and LOVE
Amen

Grace is not learned.
It is Always with us.
By Grace we Live.
And Life in Course terms
is without end
FOREVER
ALWAYS
That is GRACE.
That is Given us By Our Father...
By LOVE ITSELF.
So...in this world
whenever we find ourselves
without love...
or afraid we are alone and forsaken
Let Us
ALWAYS...REMEMBER...
The GRACE OF GOD IS WITH US ALWAYS
It is His Gift.
Grace is what makes Salvation Certain.

Holy Father,
We give Thanks
for YOUR LOVE
and the Way
we show this Thanks
Is by Loving Your Creations
Our Brother
is ONE with US
Amen

This is not our home.
We are visiting here.
So a part of us
remembers
The MAGNITUDE of the LOVE
that WE ARE.
and...
What fools these mortals be.
We come to this world
looking for our SELF.
For LOVE.
And it is not really available here.
UNLESS WE REMEMBER IT IS US.
THAT BRINGS IT

Our Relationships
are our BEST TEACHERS.
And gives us
a way of recognizing
Our Self.
By either RECOGNIZING our BROTHER,
And WHO HE IS,
Or if we are not there yet,
Shows us how our projections
of our view of ourself
is the barrier
that keeps us
from the LOVE WE ARE.
And FORGIVENESS is the Way
to undo and remove this barrier
to OUR REAL IDENTITY.
And ONLY THIS will allow
the JOY and HAPPINESS
which is our Legacy and Inheritance
to be ours.
NOTHING ELSE can...or will

When it dawned on me
that the Beauty I See in others
is actually a reflection
of my own
and of course...visa versa
That which I did not really like about others
well...that was a projection
of what I did not want to see
Within.
I remember that moment really well.
For it did bring the first tears of Happiness
to my eyes
that I ever experienced.
Because first,
I KNEW IT WAS TRUE.
And I realized...
that I did see a lot
of Beauty
in others.

Either our Brother is
"calling for Love"
And we have
an opportunity to release him
from what he thinks he is
by seeing His True Self,
Or He is Extending Love.
Which just means.
We Join
and
Be Our Self
in a way...there is no in-between

We live in two different worlds.
That is the source
of our "unhappiness"
Yet
The solution...is easy.
If we can remember
One is real
This is not...so pay it no mind.
Now when we look in the mirror
and pay it no mind
We have begun the process .

yet in a way...
when you get used to The Matrix idea,
And The Wizard of Oz,
And someone pulling all the strings
as it has been written...already
It seems that it is unfolding rather naturally
...isn't it?

"Do we understand
that this world was made
as an attack on God?"
Yes...for the most part.
If we don't see other people's guilt,
we wonder why this is happening to us.
Doesn't God love us?
And if he did...why this?
This is again projecting the guilt out
onto a God we made.
And the Bible will tell us all we need as proof
God created this world.
So...everything is in place.
Yes...sin, guilt and its punishment
are the 3 legs of the ego's foundation.

There is another scenario
which some of us do try and walk.
That is...not committing any wrongdoing
so we don't have to feel guilty
and live to please God.
Aha...this is just another form
of the same ego game.
For all it does
is to keep us seeing it in others.
Not in us.
WORSE...
It keeps us "safe and sound"
in the past, future world of the ego, mind
which is to be slave
to the ego's dictates of right and wrong
as perceived from past...thoughts and ideas
and to escape future punishment
...sounds safe...
NO WAY OUT!!!
until the person says
THERE MUST BE ANOTHER WAY...
..and that is how we all got here.

Father
We Ask that tonite...
we Open
our Spiritual Eye...
and See
with the Perception
of the Holy Spirit
for His brings Our Meaning
and
Our Identity to Us...
for this
We Give Thanks and Gratitude...
Amen

YOU ARE THE HOLY SON OF GOD HIMSELF.
You cannot suffer.
Cannot be in pain.
Cannot suffer loss.
Nor fail to do all that
Salvation asks.
Now...
That is what the
UNION of
the FATHER and SON
means
Amen.

When I brought
the dark thoughts
to the LIGHT
and ASKED HIM
to SHARE His Perception
SO I COULD SEE IT,
IT WAS VERY LAUGHABLE.
And I got to see how small
I think...in my wrong mind.
SO...PLEASE...
Take this with you...
and PRACTICE it.

THE LIGHT ...
will replace the dark...
That is a Promise...

As far as the Course is concerned
it Simply says...
Take what you can.
For we all are SO addicted
to this world's illusions...
and the Course knows this
And Gently says...
You will take whatever you can take.
Leave...and then come back for more.
So...IT IS A HIGHLY
Personalized Curriculum
Which we each take
And learn at our own pace.

Success is measured
by how we are able to move
thru this Illusion...
with all of its bumps and grinds
and Allow
our Spirit to Soar
to Show Us
the Way.

Let us Remember
Whenever we forget
To Be Gentle
with Our Self,
For
Our True Purpose...
Is to Remember
THE LOVE We ARE
and We Would
Give that Gentleness
to ALL WE SHARE
the LOVE.
Amen

May your Life be filled
with these wonderful moments
of Peace and Quiet
where your Happiness
abounds.

When two Hearts beat
as ONE.
it is already Forever!
...and a day

BOTTOM LINE.
IT'S ALL ILLUSION.
WON'T WE BE GLAD ABOUT THAT
WHEN WE WAKE UP
and LOOK AROUND
and SAY...
Geeeee whizzzzzzz
Took all that stuff personally
When we were
ALL ONE.

If you are doing your Purpose
here...
your Health will be provided for
since you do not have
to have your mind
upon your body's health...
if it is fulfilling its function.

Ohhh What a ONEderful Morning!!
Oh What a ONEderful Day!!
I 'm Feeling that old time Feeling
EveryONE's going my Way...

WAKE UP and LAUGH AT IT ALL!
This is the Message of the Course.
For if we can't laugh at it all,
or any part of it,
we are still identifying
with what we made
and not with WHO WE ARE
as God Created US!

Both in TRUST and TOLERANCE
I have found
that probably our greatest fear
is that we,
OR another,
may be out of control.
For in TRUST,
we are asked to Accept
what seems to happen...to us.
And as ACIM says...
it may seem that what you have
formerly valued
may be taken away...from you
And sometimes it is.
Yet it is thru this...that we Learn
that it had no real value at all.
It may even seem...
that we are "Losing Control".
HOWEVER...
In Truth...
We never had "control in this illusion".

And when we see our Brother
who may also "appear"
to be temporarily out of control,
our own inner belief
is reflected outside of us.
And we see
our Brother
as guilty,
being out of control.
THIS...is how TOLERANCE...
and TRUST
allows us
to Know
that this is the way of the illusion.
YET
NO HARM WILL COME TO US
in REALITY.
So...Be Gentle...and enJOY!

"Are you defending?"
Yes!
It is this false image
of one who would want
to appear
as in
control
that we defend
the shabby substitute
for The Creator
the Son of God.

Hmmmmmmmmmmmmmmmmmmm...

Let us Come with Open Minds
and Open Hearts
to Ask for Guidance
from He Who Comes to Give IT.
All that He Asks
is for our Willingness
to Listen.
And for ALL that We Hear
we are Grateful
and
Give Thanks
Amen.

Keep on Keeping ON...
Smile at the dream...
and
Ask to See it Differently!

Someone once said
understanding is the booby prize.
Understanding what the lessons say
keeps us from PRACTICING the Lesson
which is all that is ASKED.
Which is the Experience required.
The lessons do not
ask us to understand it,
or believe in it,
or to accept it.
ACIM just Asks US to do it.
To Practice the Lesson.
It is in the doing or practicing of the Lesson
that the change of mind,
the Purification of our worldly mind,
that prepares the mind for
Miracle readiness
and for Miracles.
When we are hungry...we don't try to understand
how a refrigerator works
before we open the door.
SO...I say...
Just practice the lessons,
For that is all that is Asked of US.
And SEE...
how the world lightens UP
as YOU WAKE UP WHOLE
and Perfect.

ReMember...
Your True Identity
is just a Thought away.
Yes.
We can Change our mind,
at any time.
And Awaken to the Truth.
We are
the ONE SON OF GOD
and THE EXTENDED LOVE HE IS
ALWAYS!

Life has a funny way
of playing tricks
on the unsuspecting mind.
ONLY the Awakened Mind
sees it as just a play on the senses
that believes what it sees
and thinks is real.
The "unsuspecting"
play out the forces
that they attract by those beliefs
and "Reality" takes the blame
as having dealt a bad hand
or someone is blamed
as to making it happen
or GOD is "unloving"
or how else could this happen?
A Course in Miracles
comes into this world of shadows
a Beacon...
which allows the shadows
to be brought to Light
so that the Awakened SON
can see the folly
of the games he fabricated
to "replace" Unconditional Love
as if it could be "replaced"!

LOVE SPRINGS ETERNAL!!!
It's OUR NATURAL INHERITANCE
and its ABUNDANCE
is without limits,
and opposite the "laws" of this world...
THE MORE YOU GIVE...
the MORE YOU HAVE
SO SHARE YOURSELF...
and Extend Your Loving Thoughts
for the ONE you Give to...
is Your Self...
Think about it!

Yet knowing the Course
is not the same as Walking the Course.
So, this is a time to be Vigilant
for our Purpose
and Commitment to Awaken
which is our Only Function here.
Whenever we are "sucked" into the illusion
we need to ASK AGAIN
to SEE IT Differently
or else...
we have failed "temporarily"
to carry out our Function.
When this happens
what's to do?
BEGIN AGAIN.
YET, NEVER LET US FORGET...
what looks like a failure...
or a step backwards...
is another STEP FORWARD....
on the Path...we ALL WALK...
for lest we forget...
IT IS WRITTEN...
and we are playing out the parts
we Agreed to play.

We focus on that
which will bring us
what is valuable...
and to sort out that
which has no value...
and to
CHOOSE AND SHARE
the Valuable.
For only by Sharing...
do we INCREASE anything
that has Value.

We harbor
two different
and
OPPOSITE
thought systems
that cannot co-exist...witihin our mind...
and we keep them separate.
This is what the Course calls disassociation.
Which is a distorted process of thinking
whereby two systems are maintained.
When in REALITY
they cannot co-exist.
UNLESS...
they are brought together
they will stay...
in opposition to each other.
And though...it doesn't look like a big deal
it is the
VERY BASIS
of sacrifice.
For even though
TRUTH IS...
it can either be recognized...or NOT recognized.

And if we keep
the two thought systems
apart,
that is our way of defending
what we know.
We need to bring them together.
For then...
ONLY ONE WILL REMAIN.
I call it the
UNION OF THE FATHER AND THE SON .

Tonite
We place the emphasis on the DO's
since as the Course says
Holy Spirit...always Guides Us
by saying...Do this...or Do that.
Only ego...who always speaks first
says...don't do this or don't do that.
So with that reminder...
and the 5 DO's to do,
I have this one caveat.
One "DO NOT"
which appears to be a trap we all fall into
is the desire to understand
how Miracles Work.
and my reply
is you DO NOT have to.
For as the Course itself says
there is a lot we will not be
able to understand...NOW..
given the limitations
of our mind's ability to see the WHOLE.
Yet We can AWAKEN WHOLE
if we follow the 5 DO's.

The 5 DO'S are as follows:
We will take the first 2 together
1. Take time out...and...Be with Him
Who is Our Father.
Leave the world outside
and the Time you take
out of your busy day
to spend in Quiet...and Silence
and Be with Your Father
is Your Decision
that This is what YOU WANT.
What You Choose,
and what you WANT...
What you Ask For...
is Given You.
And YOUR CHOICE...determines Your Goal.
That handles time...
Now Space....
EXTEND Your Self.
The Bridge you Build
between you and Your Brother,
which appears to be Extended outward,
as you See Your Brother As Yourself
is ALSO
the Bridge you are Building WITHIN
to Your TRUE SELF.

For in Reality...there is no...In or OUT
For in WHOLENESS
direction and space is...
meaningless.
The next 2 DO's have to do with YOU
as Cause
and Whole in All you do.
In everything
that you can remember TO DO...
practice Being WHOLE.
For to see only in part,
which is what we all see,
this part...that part...
their side...our side...
him or me...
my way...or their way...
is a kind of partition...or separateness...
which is what this world is designed for.
Ask again
To see it as WHOLE.
To See the WHOLENESS.
Which is True Sight.
For truly we do not see at all
with our body's eyes.
So a gentle way of Correcting our vision
for True Sight
is to ASK AGAIN
to see THE WHOLE.

It is our ASKING
that does this for us.
For we are then saying
that we truly do not know.
We do NOT understand,
which is the truth...we do not.
Not knowing
prepares us
FOR Knowing.
The 4th Do
is Lesson 30
which is to see God in everything
because God...is in my mind.
Which is the TRUTH.
With that as a RE-MIND-ER...
We can begin to be the Loving Being that we are
and begin to RE-MEMBER
our true IDENTITY
which IS LOVE
which we threw away.
Being Cause is also the way to include
The subchapter "Responsibility for Sight"
which simply says...
"I am responsible for what I see
and I choose the feelings I experience
and I decide upon the goal I would achieve.
And EVERYTHING that seems to happen to me
I ask for...and receive as I have asked".

THIS IS TRULY EMPOWERING!
For it puts you at CAUSE.
And possibly for the first time
in the dream we dream together
we see ourselves...as the dreamer
and NOT as a victim.
Once this shift takes place
we can begin to See
what it is that we do
and why we do what we do
to our Self.
This is where change can be made.
Change in our MIND
by Choosing Again
What is Real...and what is not.
Here is the only place where change
is MEANINGFUL.
To change our THOUGHT System
and the Thoughts we think.

Finally...the 5th Do.
ASK!
Whenever in doubt
and let's say...we seem to be there a lot
since we seem to be caught up in all forms
of doubt and confusion
these forms come in all sizes and shapes,
But they are all the same.
The multitude of forms of fear
and belief in the impossible...our separation
looks like blame, shame, guilt,
anger, jealousy, resentment,
and depression.
The idea of feeling less than whole...vulnerable...
imperfect.
These are just some of the forms
of doubt...about our SELF...it is called ...
SELF DOUBT.
When in doubt...
JUST ASK!
ASK AGAIN of the HOLY SPIRIT
to SEE IT AS HE SEES IT.
FOR HE SEES THE WHOLE.
He is never fooled by our impossible dream
which we made to deceive ourselves.

The Course says,
"there crept a tiny, mad idea, at which the Son of God
remembered not to laugh" (T-27. VIII.6).
Which makes the anecdote
simple...
WAKEUP and Laugh...at it all!
However, sometimes this virtual reality world
gets "a bit complex".
So when we "refuse to laugh"
at something...anything...
it doesn't matter what...
Remember...
We have placed this "whatever"
before our Self
and as such
it is a "graven image"...
an idol which we see
as our Salvation...
Even though Our Salvation
is Guaranteed by God!

This is an "attack" on our Creator...
as if this is possible, thus,
it is an attack on our Self.
For it can only be ourself that we attack.
So look around and see what you hold dear
in this world
And recognize
that somehow...
somewhere...
we have together placed this idol which is
"valueless"
on a pedestal
and made it valuable.

We All have a lot in common.
That is the basis of ACIM,
our ONENESS.
Of course
We are speaking of our ONE Creator,
and the ONE MIND
which
We All Share with Him
Together.

THE BEAUTY OF A COURSE IN MIRACLES
is that it gently reminds us
that we have
another Voice
Within.
Maybe not as loud
and as demanding of our attention,
though
ONE
that KNOWS WHO WE ARE
and Sees US
and the People in our life
differently
then the teaching of the ego.

Listen,
You should know,
I am only speaking to myself.
You just happen to be there...
and allow me to say all this
to MYSELF.
so THANKS.

When we Awaken and Heal
we will look back
and smile at this stuff.
Stuff we thought so important.
How can we finally
"lay down,
even this book,
and come
with open hands and open mind
to our Father"
When we dream only of more books?
If we are Healed
we are not Healed alone.
This is our function.
It is Simple...not complex.
Let Us Ask for Peace NOW!
And mean it.
And everything that we would
see in this world of differences
will be meaningless.

FATHER
Let us not ever forget
that though we may have
temporarily lost our mind
...as IF that was possible...:-)
WE HAVE NEVER LOST YOUR LOVE.
So in REMEMBRANCE
of YOUR ETERNAL LOVE for US
We give you this "timeless Gift"
of Choosing to BE HAPPY,
and not right,
about the Idea
YOU ARE WITH US
ALWAYS
until that day
We AWAKEN in YOUR ARMS
as We are NOW
and Know
Our Self
in the Loving
ONENESS YOU CREATED US
Amen

We are in a new Millennium
One that Promises to Bring US HOME.
A Journey
that may be slow and tortuous
or one that travels
at the Speed of Light and Thought!
The Path we Choose
to walk here
makes ALL the difference.
Thus Miracles Happen
THRU YOU!

CHOOSE TO EXTEND LOVE TO ALL
and Let Your Light Shine
without boundaries,
without specialness,
like a LIGHTHOUSE.
And you have kept
the Ancient Promise
we all have made
in that distant ancient time
TO LOVE
as Your Father Loves YOU...
without the limits
that the illusion of separation
may temporarily blind us with.
See that What We Give,
We Give to Our Self
so We may Know
that Love Lives in US
as US!

TEACH LOVE...
For that is
WHO YOU ARE!

As A Course in Miracles points out...
We are slave
to the dictates of
the ego we made...
as a shabby substitute
for our TRUE SELF.
It is this dream-like slavery ...
that ACIM would have us
HEAL and AWAKEN from...
and it is this...
IDEA of FREEDOM....
"the escape from bondage"
which we celebrate

Wonderful things
are
Happening... :-)

When we say
We are ALL HERE
WE MEAN ALL.
Those that are here...
in body form....
those that ...
were in body form....
and who used their time...
to learn the lessons
we are all required...
to let go of this ego world
we made...
and WAKE UP
to our
IMMORTAL LOVING SELF
Created as an Idea
in the Mind of God...
where we remain
Now...
and will Know
upon Awakening

Yes, and those that have passed on,
yet touched our lives
in many ways,
provided lessons for us
to advance our own learning.
For they So Loved Us
that They Lived their Life
for us to Learn of OUR SELF.
Just as We will Give to them.
by our own Learning
and Awakening.
And hasten the day
when we WILL be Free
of our illusions of limitations
and separation,
and the multitude of forms of fear
will be cast out forever
by the Perfect Love We Are
for WE ARE ONE!

....and for ALL of this
We are Grateful
to ALL in our Life
and
to Our Father
for His Divine Plan
which Lives in
ALL of US

Let Your Light Shine Ahead
and include
All you meet.
And in the event
the illusion
seems real...
LIGHTEN UP
and LAUGH!!
For laughter
is the sign
of recognizing
the illusion .

Richard Bach,
author of
"Johnathan Livingston Seagull"
and "Illusions"
wrote another book called
"There Is No Such Place
as Far Away"
In it he says,
No matter how far
you "think" you are separated
from someone
by time or distance
as it may "appear"
in this illusion,
the experience you have
the moment
you think of them...
they are with you.
Thus...death is not real.

The Spirit and Idea Live
Forever!
As any ACIMer knows.
I extend that Loving Thought to All
Let us Remember
Our Loved Ones
that we "believe" are separated
from us by either
"time or distance".
See them as their
Loving Perfect Self
as the Son of God
who Lives Forever
and we are
ONE WITH THEM
GOD IS LOVE
and Created US
as LOVE...
LIFE is Given without end!

Then why ask...What is it for?
It either serves
the Holy Spirit Purpose
or the ego's purpose.
And only ONE WAY
is worth seeing.
The other
has no meaning...in REALITY.
The body can either serve the Holy Spirit
or ego.
CHOOSE!
Can say that about everything
in this 4D world.
One serves to be
FREE of this world.
The other serves
to keep you prisoner
in this world.
CHOOSE!

It's like you are tip-toeing
thru this virtual reality world...
kinda like Alice... in Wonderland.
You look at something
and it screams at you
Pick me up!
And hold me high
Place me on your altar!
Sooner or later...
Alice...WISES UP
And sees what
the stuff is for
and asks
To see it differently .
107
IT ALL CLEARS UP
SOONER...
OR LATER.

I am reminded
of my favorite ACIM metaphor,
that for me is the
quintessential story
that captures the
Spirit and Idea...behind the Course.
It is a story that I heard
Marianne Williamson relay...
about an advanced group of
Miracle Students
who met regularly in
Northern California.
It seems that they were discussing
a few paragraphs in the closing chapters
of the Text.
Whereas, half of the group
interpreted the meaning
of the passage one way,
the other half saw it differently.
This brought on a lengthy discussion
that went nowhere and
left the room divided.
Finally, one of the group turned to
Bill Thetford who was a part of the group...
yet had said nothing
through all of this, saying,
"Bill, What do you think the Course is saying...
after all, you were there with Helen,
when she received this".

Bill thought about it for a few moments...
and said...
"I would tear this page right out of the book,
for anything that
separates the Equal Sons of God
...is not worth discussing."
To what avail is this discussion,
whether it be for "accuracy, legal or personal
reasons".
Always ask of all things...
What is it for?
What value would anything
that serves to further separate the Equal Sons of
God...
be?
What would our Older Brother
who Gives us this Course, say ...or think,
when he tells us to
AWAKEN from this dream.
Why perpetuate this dream...
when everything but
"forgiveness"
will only produce
multiple more dreams
for the Sonship
to sleep in.

Let Us Ask for Peace NOW
and mean it!
And everything that we would see
in this world of differences
will be meaningless.
Let this year be different
by making it all the same.
I Trust My Brothers
who are
ONE
with me.

Kindness is a facet
of the LOVE that WE ARE!
Extending Our Love to ALL in our life,
including the person you meet
only once for a few short minutes,
is WALKING THE WALK of the COURSE.
We can read...chat...attend groups...
and ask questions...in order to learn...
and all of this is what we do...
when we "talk the talk"
as a way of Teaching that part of us
that needs to "learn" or re-member
the Truth about our Self
and our Brothers and Sisters
who share this dream and world
we made as a temporary place...
a "virtual reality"
of our Self...
on a "grand" scale.

LOVE cannot be taught
for that is
WHO WE ARE!
The blocks to Extending Love
is our fear(s).
Let's use today
and everyday
to re-member
WHO WE ARE
by Extending
random acts of LOVE.
to ALL WE MEET
for nothing will dissolve
the forms of fear
that keep us bound
faster.
As lesson 30 says...
"God is in everything I See...
because God is in MY MIND"
For we are either Host to LOVE
or hostage to the ego we made
Choose!

LOVE IS IN THE AIR...
and in
OUR MINDS
the Eternal Spring.
is
HERE and NOW
USE IT!

Say Your
Prayers.
115
Each of us
makes a Major difference
when we both
learn and teach
the Course principles.
For this is the way
it begins to show up
in the world
on the Silver Screen,
TV and wind its way
into the popular culture.
For Waking UP is a lot easier
if you first know
you are asleep
and dreaming something
that "seems" real.
And We Each and ALL
have the Power
to Forget,
Forgive
and Awaken!
116
Thank God
We can afford
to Laugh NOW!
For those who Walk the Path...
and know they look at the unreal ....
they are the Truly Blessed!
Yet we are

ALL BLESSED.
Since whether we know
that what this world is for
or not,
we can be Fully Comforted
by the Comforter
Who Quietly Says
Fear not.
For what you look upon
is not real
and YOU ARE!
That which is Real
cannot be destroyed
that which is unreal,
doesn't exist...
herein lies
the Peace of God.

Yes...
THANK GOD
we can afford to Laugh NOW!
And fool ourselves
no longer
with the dreams
of separation
and abandonment.
It's time to WAKE-UP
and Remember
Our Loving Father
WHO IS WITH US ALWAYS...
And to
Forgive our Self
and this world we made,
for "believing"
differently
...if even only for a moment!

MIRACLES
are
for
SHARING!

And we ARE AFRAID.
So the first line says
ONLY THE SANE
can look upon terror and violence
with Compassion.
For that mind is without fear
for it HAS FORGIVEN
and UNDERSTANDS
that killing LOVE and God is not possible.
So it CAN EMPATHIZE.
There was the question
to whether stepping aside and being NEUTRAL
is the same as Apathy.
Since apathy brings on more guilt,
and that is NOT the intended result,
the difference between apathy...
and ASKING the Holy Spirit to intervene...
because we do not understand
what we see
is that we are actively asking to
ACCESS our Right Mind
which is here for our Use.
Yet, unless we disconnect from the impulses
and thoughts of the past...and the ego
we are going nowhere
and stay within the dream
THAT WE HAVE COME HERE TO AWAKEN FROM

Let us Come Together
and Open Our Minds...
to Remember...That
Love is What Created US
as Loving...
Kind...
Helping...
and Perfect
and That
ALL of our Brothers...and Sisters...
everywhere...
are as WE ARE....
Created
by the Same Love
that Created US ALL...
Amen

For we do not know
what Compassion is.
Yes, we see suffering...
and violence...
and we take sides.
In taking sides...
we are in the domain of the ego.
Who only takes sides
to keep the separation
alive and well.

The ego's interpretation
of empathy,
is always used to form
a special relationship
in which the
suffering is shared.
The ego always uses
joining in and seeing suffering.
And out of our
"human compassion and pity"
for the sufferer
or the victim...
and looking as to
who the guilty are...
and where the blame
shall be laid...
SEEKS ONLY TO WEAKEN US FURTHER...
Keeping us solidly
in the dream.
We are hooked
thinking that
we have done
all that we can.

Perception by any member
of the Sonship
of "differences"...
reflects the belief in the separation...
or conflict or "unequal" or divided self
or split mind...
which the Course speaks of.
It can be said...however,
that darkness represents
the "sleeping mind"
which the Course certainly says,
we are dreaming in a deep sleep
And the Light
is that which we Know
when we Awaken.
So the contract
between asleep and Awake
is certainly part of this world.

Of course...those that are temporarily
more Awake than their Brothers,
who still see the world as all there is,
therefore in a deeper sleep...
can See their Brothers
as not in the darkness...
but see them as Awakened.
This perception
which must come from
the Healed Mind...
that sees no separation
and no differences...
Sees ALL as the SAME.

Let US come
with Open Hearts
and
empty minds
to ASK For HIS PEACE
so we may Be Filled
With His Understanding
and For this we
Give OUR THANKS
and Gratitude
Amen

Dear Father
WE GIVE THANKS
for
YOUR PEACE
and
LOVE
Amen

YET
IT is WITHIN
that
WE MUST LOOK
for
WHO WE ARE.

I am reminded at this time
of the subchapter
"The Responsibility for Sight".
This is clearly
the opposite of the ego's teachings
or the teachings of this world.
It puts us at CAUSE
with nobody else to blame.
And
not effect of a world
that seems to be doing
it to us as helpless victims.
SOOOOOOOO...
As Einstein said,
"If the idea is not absurd...
there is no hope for it."
It is absurd...
yet FORGIVENESS teaches us
to release us BOTH
from what I mistakenly made.
And NOW I CAN
unmake it.

SO, it seems clear
that the first thing
we need to say is...
I KNOW NOTHING.
For anything that we think after that...
tells us what the ego would have us believe
and that will
NOT
give us
The PEACE we seek.

After the evening
I kinda looked at my own life
and realized...
that just about everything in it
that seemed to be a "cause" of
pain and unhappiness
came from
"wanting to be right"
and not wrong.
And of course
when you are wrong...it is painful.
Then I took another look
at what was the foundations
of being right
and realized that in this world...
we worship being right.
Being right
in any field of endeavor
is what it's all about.
You might say...
as the famous football coach said...
winning isn't everything...
its the only thing.
And of course...when someone wins.
someone loses.

Let's face it
we live in a world,
perhaps a virtual world,
where we worship...being right.
Winning...and not losing.
So...I looked a little deeper into the idea.
Where does being right come from...for me?
Welllll...
Guess what??
We have a "friend"
whose only function is
pointing out right
and wrong.
You know when someone says...
They are looking for Mr. Right...or Miss Right...
Guess what???
We are "married to him or her...already."
Now...one of the characteristics of that friend
is to "not be wrong."
So...even if you are "right"...guess what???
We are simultaneously ..."wrong".
Why???
Because it keeps you stuck
in a world...of right and wrong.

And while we try
real hard to be right
we never realize
what we are doing
is just hanging out
in a world
where the rules...
of right and wrong
are being preached
and practiced.
And that is where
we have given up our
True Identity.
That is the cost...
the heavy cost...the gravity...
when LIGHT
without limit
adopts a world
with limits.

Okay!!
There is no right and wrong.
Easy to say,
however,
in this world
not easy to practice
unless...
you are doing your lessons of course.

And
NOBODY
outside of our SELF
is the cause
of our unhappiness.
IT IS OUR
WANTING TO BE RIGHT
about the way things are
which keeps us
TIED DOWN
to the friend
who dictates right and wrong.

In this world we are using
parts.
For this world is a world
of parts
in which we see ourselves
A-PART
from others.
That is what the belief in separation
is about...
the idea...of being apart...
or separate.
So...we show up in these bodies
which in this world
LOOKS a-part.
Are we beginning to get the idea
that even though we talk about this stuff
this virtual stuff...
because we are so mired in the stuff
it takes some real
DILIGENCE
to WISE UP
and WAKE UP!!!!

So don't do
what you don't
enjoy doing.

It is
VERY CLEAR
that striving
outside of ourselves
or looking for Happiness
outside
WILL FAIL.
And whatever idol
we choose
for
our happiness...
will fail for sure.

For we are in a virtual world.
And what keeps us
"FOCUSED"
on what the world teaches us
is the addiction
to our "friend"...
the ego
that we made
to teach us
what is right
and wrong
or to point out
what is wrong about others.
Kind of a survival mechanism.
For that is what it is
in a world
where
survival of the fittest
is the theme.

For in a world
of parts...
and not WHOLENESS
there is always
lack.
Different forms of time and space...
of limits.
LIGHT
has no limits
or lack
IT IS WHOLE.

Let's face it...
the COURSE says
WE DID THIS
to our SELF
because
we had an insane belief
that we could be "a part"
from Our Creator.
And that His Will
is different from our Will.
And we WANTED
to be "right" about it.
Being right
about being "a part"
WHEN WE ARE WHOLE.
so we "made" a world
where "PARTIAL Thinking"
passes for thought.
NO WONDER...the COURSE...says
what you call thought...
is NOT thought at all.
What we need to begin to do
is TO USE WHOLE THOUGHT.
WHOLE FOOD FOR THOUGHT.
And where else can you find this stuff????????
IN THE LESSONS
ACIM LESSONS 1-365

It is a wonderful way of
Turning on the Light switch.
To think of the
ONES WE LOVE.
That it is also the way to
INCLUDE
our Brothers
with which we
still have
grievances with
By Thinking of
A LOVED ONE
and Let the Light
that Radiates from us
and Surrounds
the One we Love
to INCLUDE
the Brother who seems
to be standing
outside
the Light.

This is the Miracle...
Where A LIGHT...
that we thought was only
Good for ONE
INCLUDES ALL.
FOR THE LIGHT
knows no separation
or limitations.
It is our "using our Mind"
to think of the grievances
we have with Our Brother
that keeps us from Seeing the Light
That is ALWAYS THERE.
So...As Jesus would say...
EXTEND YOUR LIGHT AND LOVE.
That is the way TO HAVE MORE LIGHT.
Since the littleness...
that we use to occupy our mind's thoughts
will just disappear into the nothingness
that they are
Leaving us
AS A TOWER OF LIGHT... :-)
Birthing the CHRIST
becomes the Path
that is EASIEST
to follow.

FOR
WHAT WE ARE
and
WHAT WE HAVE.
Is Given By You
TO US FREELY
WITH ALL YOUR LOVE
and FOR THIS
WE ARE GRATEFUL NOW...
and ALWAYS
Amen

WHAT YOU HAVE NOW
and NOW
and NOW
is what you bring with
you.

Let us REMEMBER
to Count the Blessings
of what we
HAVE NOW.
For what we bring to the NEW
WILL ONLY
MULTIPLY.
And this is a good time
NOW.
To Give our
Thanks
and
Gratitude
for these
Blessings.

As we all know...
Lesson 1 says
"Everything I see in this room...
out that window...and in the world
is meaningless.
Of course...
we do resist getting that.
So we do
as good students
move on to the next lesson
which does go on to say
that WE
gave everything we see
here and out there
the meaning it has for us.
The very first lesson
says it all
if we are willing to get
IT
we could start
Laughing
right then
OR NOW!
For it is the ultimate cosmic joke

I am laughing
because you have touched
on the hardest part
of trying to
LIVE the Course.
As much as we do know
all the principles of the Course,
and look to Apply
the Lessons of the Course
on a daily basis
the "ability" to let go of the past
and to "recognize" that none
of my past thoughts
mean anything
or putting it simply...
are meaningless
and
THIS MOMENT
is ALL THERE IS..

Let us be Grateful for
THIS MOMENT of PEACE
in which we Can Know
Our Self
and the Love of Our Father.
It's not easy.
YET...This is our function.
And only this will work.
For anything other than this
just invites more illusion
ONLY
by breaking the chain
of the past brought into the present
so that there is no present
only past
CAN WE FIND THE SALVATION...
and HEALING
that ACIM SPEAKS of.
Sooooooooo...
Place the focus
where it belongs

I also thought your idea...
that there is only "me"
is terrific...
For that is True.
There is nobody out there.
What ever we see...It is US
It is me.
Hard one to get...YET TRUE
And the faster we get
It's Truth
the Easier this gets.
For it puts US at Cause.
And not effect.
YES.
There are no coincidences.
IT IS ALL WRITTEN.
And we are playing out our parts.
And we can LEARN
from EVERY ONE
that We let into our Life.
You can SAY
YES or NO.
SAY YESSSSSSSSS!!!
:-)

It is really...
a BIGGIE...
to give up your identity.
How our grievances
are only an aspect
of our wanting to be right
about something
and the cost
it has on us...
Our health
and most important
the delay
or the cost
in wasting time
for
our Awakening...
to fulfill
Our Purpose of being here.

A COURSE IN MIRACLES
SAYS
You have a choice.
YOU CAN EITHER BE
HAPPY
or
RIGHT.
Choose one.
For you cant have both.
I think that is the question
we face
each and every time
we take a position
in opposition
to a brother
and feel that
we
are
right.

This is an opportunity
of letting go
of the past
and awakening to
The Real World.
Where the grievances
from our dream state
do not exist.

Let us
TOGETHER...then conclude
with a Moment of Prayer
for our
Oneness
and Awakening
and for
PEACE...
for
ALL WORLDWIDE
Amen

Our Function
is
to not only
to refuse to listen...
TO WITHDRAW
our belief in it.
For it is unbelievable.
Remember...
If we can see
ANY PART
of the ego's thoughts
as
"WHOLLY insane, delusional or undesirable..."
we have
Correctly seen it all.
And
FREES
us to
SEE
WHOLENESS

You can only bring
the dark cornerstones
to the Light.
Not visa versa.
And when you bring
that which is
"nothing"
into
the Light
it disappears
into the
nothingness
that it is.

It says
just as you are about
to enter into a Holy Relationship,
the ego would teach...
to enter into a relationship where
you can have illusions
that you do not share...with the other...
The Text says...HEAR THIS NOT.
For...as you point out...
the ego would have us
listen to its...direction.
When I read this
I remember
I thought...
AHA!!!
I guess
I am not ready to be healed.
For it is true.
We say we wish to be healed
but we continue
to follow the dictates and principles
of the ego.
Which is our own
way of saying...
LATER...
to Healing

I was thinking of how the Course
speaks to us of our INVULNERABILITY.
And of course
the ego only speaks of our vulnerability...
our fragility.
Which your ego...immediately...took offense to
and spoke to the "idea of you"
that is vulnerable...and ready to "hurt".
You may not be upset for the reason you think.
Certainly...
if we don't know ourself...
this vulnerable self...will be "upset".
And IF we are not ready to be HEALED,
---> To "Know Your Self"
Then of course we are in fear.
For we are vulnerable...
a speck of dust
in a chaotic world
where we don't know what anything is for.
And certainly don't know ...what tomorrow brings.
This is the world of the ego.
We have one problem.
And that is not really a problem.
So the solution...is SIMPLE.

CHANGE TEACHERS...
and not listen to the bidding...
of the ego...
UNLESS...
You are willing to look in the mirror
and say...
I'm just not ready right now...to wake up."
The Choice is
UP TO US
in this Lifetime
or next.
It's on Our Watch!

The Course starts out...
There is only LOVE...and fear.
SO LOVE...has no opposite.
For fear is nothing more
than...un-love.
Fear = lack of love.
THAT IS WHAT WE ALL BELIEVE IN.
What we cherish
because we MADE IT.
A world...that says
that there is
NO Love
or NO...God.
And OF COURSE
we have peopled it...from Central Casting
with LOTS of evidence that this is true
or else...how could the ego,
who is our defender and champion,
of the fragile...easily hurt those of us,
that means anyone in a body,
who "lacks"...LOVE...or in other words
Doesn't know WHO THEY ARE...
AS LOVE ITSELF.
And Perfect Love
casts out "lack of love".
For ALL there is...
is LOVE...
and HIS EXTENSIONS...THE SONSHIP... US.

The Path we walk
is a very
Perfect Path.
There are no accidents.
For if we can stay with OUR SELF,
who is our brother,
STAY the COURSE
There is a Healing
that Gives
US THE LIGHT
to SHINE THE WAY
that others may follow.
SOMEHOW,
it all works,
by the Grace of God.
On that Path...
where so many do fall
We have the Power to Raise Us UP!
There is a real Rhyme...
even in all this madness.

It is obvious
that when we let go
of all of our
misperceptions
and illusions
of this world...
and correct our Vision
as our Older Brother Jesus did
We Will also be Healed.
And Love...
which is there
already
will Radiate.
And with it
the Gratitude
of our ONENESS
with Our Creator...
and With ALL...LIFE.
It is this Healing
and Understanding and KNOWLEDGE
of our ONENESS
that ...we have as our Purpose.
We can wait until then...
OR...begin practicing NOW
By choosing...
to Walk in Gratitude...NOW.
Even...if we don't fully
SEE our Oneness
NOW.

There is more than 1 way
to understand.
Some will find it in this course
and in the exercises
that we do today.
So ...the Course is saying...
that doing the Lessons...does work.
And is one of the ways
we can Understand
and KNOW our Invulnerability.
Jon Mundy,
one of the Course Teachers
used to say...
IF one dies before he dies...
then he doesn't' die...when he dies.
It's an old Tibetan saying.

Just about everything we do
and get attached to
in this dream we made...together
is to forget our self...
OUR ONE SELF
The one we kinda left at the Door
when we came into this world.
And the ONE
which we have...forgotten...
while we are tempted by everything here
that appears
to have more worth
than our ONE SELF.
So this is the Way back to
SELF WORTH
where we recognize and Realize
that nothing...nothing here...
can ever be more than the light of a candle
when seen in the
LIGHT of THE SON.

Don't hold on too tight...
in fact
Let Go
and let it be.
165
We are the dreamer
of the world of dreams.
No other cause it has, nor ever will.
Together
We can remember to Awaken
from this dream...this world
we made.
And refuse
to believe the dream
we made
as anything ...
but a dream.

The procedure
that we use
to attain that
Peace...
and Quiet Mind
is not important.
What is ...
is to
ATTAIN IT.

Peace of Mind
is the
Key to the Kingdom.
For without it
we cannot enter.
So this is something
we all need to address
and ASK...to see
What Holy Spirit
ASKS
us to do
to Achieve
this
Quietness.

It has been pointed out
that ACIM
is a highly
individualized Course.
And each of us has a path
and a role.
I am saying
that however
you come
to that Quiet Mind,
so you can Listen to
THE VOICE OF GOD,
whatever it is for you...
and for me...
is what is required.
Doing the lessons... is what we all do
Probably that is the best place to start

Hdfishman: Alden...:-) it seems appropriate ..that after SO MUCH LIGHT
Hdfishman: is shed here...and Keeps Shining...
Hdfishman: that the idea of the ego...would come up...
Hdfishman: i especially like the Idea that you put forth...
Hdfishman: of taking on the New Purpose in our life...
Hdfishman: an avocation or vocation...of Extending Light...
Alden7: Yes
Hdfishman: ...my query...is..
Hdfishman: how does the ongoing dialog which the ego has...
Hdfishman: on a continuous basis...
Hdfishman: get sidetracked...by adopting this new Purpose?
Hdfishman: done
Alden7: It occurs naturally as soon as you no longer can stand it
Hdfishman: im there now
170
Happy Awakenings...and Lots of Laughter!!!
Love Always
171
ACIM lessons...why do them?
Well...the Course would say...
"Because you said you would".
And this is True.
Required means
that sooner or later
We all will Heal.
We always mean

Heal our Mind.
And the Way or Path
to Healing
is

the gentle shift
and change
in the way we see things.
And the Lessons Is the Way
for us Who practice ACIM.

Possibly I was fortunate.
When I first started out doing the Course
before I bought the books,
someone sitting right next to me,
actually a stranger
who I had not known,
and never seen again...after that day...
said...Buy the books
and just do the Lessons.
So...I did just that.
Did not open the Text
which I would have
probably had a real problem with.
And just did the Lessons
which I loved.
Did the first 50 Lessons in about 50 days.
Every one of the Lessons
were Easy...
Simple...
and made a lot of
sense to me.

I also was fortunate enough
to have a Teacher
early in my ACIM life.
His name was Paul Steinberg
who said...
The Course is actually the Lessons.
All 365 of them.
The Text
is the intellectual abstraction
of the Course.
Now whether his telling me that
influenced the way I see them today
or from experience I have found this
to be true...
The Course...is the Experience...
and the Text...,
kind of explains
what the Experience is about.

What I have found personally
in doing the lessons is
that if you are doing the Lessons
in a regular and disciplined way
that "life" begins to shift for you.
So that whatever Lesson you are doing
"somehow"
the events and people
and experiences
mirror the Lesson you are doing.
VERY STRANGE...yet true.

The Lessons
allow you to enter a state
that today's neural scientists
would call an "Alpha state".
This is a desirable place
to go and be.
It frees you
from outside influences
and allows your
Inner Being
to Awaken
and Shine.
So...a regular diet
of Lessons
is going to
place your mind
in the most
Peaceful environment
that it can be
while you are
walking thru
this world.

I kind of call Lessons 1 and 365
the Alpha and the Omega.
Since Lesson 1 says...
it is all meaningless...
and Lesson...365...
Calls on our Comforter
and says
PLEASE...lead the way...
for I would Follow you.
Certainly...for I do not know
what any of this
meaningless stuff
is for.
So PLEASE...
give me the words...
Thoughts...and Peace...
that I would have.
I usually ALWAYS...do this Lesson
whenever
I know I am
entering into the Unknown...
and in this world...
IT IS ALL UNKNOWN.

One of the best ideas
that I can share with you
in doing the lessons...
What I found...was WONDERFUL...
was ...while moving thru the day...
and something would come up...
and I could see my ego
coming on strong...
and upset...was in the air...
and I started to react to whatever
it was out there...
I would say...
LET ME DO MY LESSON INSTEAD!
And I tell you...
that is the best medicine for handling anything
that comes up in this world.
BAR NONE!!!
For immediately...what we are doing...
instead of reacting...
with our reactive ego/mind
to whatever seems
to be disturbing our Peace
or have us identify with our "mis-identity"

What we are doing and saying is NO...
It's almost like
"say NO to the ego Hdfishman"
As soon as we get into doing the Lesson
we have for that day
there is immediate benefit
As you go within...to that Peaceful place.
For that is where all Lessons take you.
And if you are doing your Lesson correctly
everything around you
will begin to look differently
and whatever appeared to be there
as an attack
somehow...
is seen differently
And I tell you...
It's a WONDERFUL FEELING

Yes...
until ACIM.
all that we are given to look at
or work with
is the concept that this world is
which is based on specialness
and separation.
The Course
give us another World
to look at
which is based
on its ONENESS
and Connectedness
and Perfection
so that we can finally SEE.

There are
no solutions
to what the world
presents us with.
There is only the
PRAYER to
AWAKEN NOW.
That is the
ONLY SOLUTION.
And that is what the
TEACHERS of GOD
are here to do.

Whenever 2 or More
are Gathered in His Name
He is Here with US.
He will Extend His Love
Through Us
As We Open Our Minds
and ASK
for the PEACE of GOD.
For that is
ALL that is required
to Enter The Kingdom
which is OUR HOME
LOVE ITSELF

Love without fear
does not see differences
separation...
or specialness.
LOVE JUST EXTENDS...
FREELY
It withholds nothing.
Every Gift IT has
is Given Freely.
This is
WHO WE TRULY ARE.

Whatever
the perception
and thought
that we have,
no matter how strongly
we may believe in it,
if its expression
brings about
any differences
and further separates
it has no value whatsoever.
For in essence...
its only purpose
was to further separate
and keep
LOVE
from Knowing
His OWN SELF.
For LOVE...
does not see differences
or separation
anywhere.

If
ALL you see
is LOVE
then TRULY
You are Extending
YOUR LOVE
and YOUR SELF

Where
there is
PERFECT LOVE
there cannot be
anything else.
So that is why
this Course
is about
Self Healing
for the only one we need to heal
is our self.

Love is already Present.
We are just not aware of it
since we have blocked ourselves from it
by building a formidable wall
of fearful decisions.
The first page
of the introduction to ACIM says this,
and the rest of the course
is about
learning to undo
that wall
which we built.
The wall of course is within our minds.
The Lessons
are simple...easy...
ways of shifting the way we see things
so that the wall is not so formidable
so thick...
so "impenetrable"
and to start to see ..
that what we thought was real...
is possibly and is
illusions
of our mind
that we have invited in.

Instead of reaching
for something
outside of our self,
with the perception that
God is a goal
that once I clear out
the obstacles in my life,
I can finally reach,
it simply says...
THE LOVE OF GOD HIMSELF
is in Your Mind
and we have a Choice
of how we want to see
anything.

One of my favorite expressions
is IYSIYGI.
Which translates to = If You Spot It You Got It.
So whether you are standing
in front of a mirror
or Your Brother...
What You see...there...
tells you which teacher
you are Listening to
at that moment.
If you don't like what you see...
Change Your Teacher.

Ahhh...
the NOW...
is WONDERFUL

That is all
anyone can ask...
PEACE NOW...
and now
and now
and...
There is a place...
within our Mind...
that is there...
ALWAYS.

This is how the
Powerful Mind
of THE Son of God works.
Think a Thought...
and you have it.
CAUSE and effect.
However...
as ACIM points out...
the idea that made this world
was "causeless"
since it had no basis in Reality.
And therefore without effects.
And the idea
of the belief in the separation
between Creator and Created
never happened.
That doesn't mean
that the Son cannot dream
of its effects...
and "think"
the dream
is real.

An Idea
cannot leave its source.
So this world,
which we dream in
is not where we are...in Course Terms.
Our only function here
is the Atonement.
The undoing or Forgiveness
Of what is unreal.
The Great Awakening which we are in
happens as quickly
as we CHOOSE.

Home...
is the only Idea
that is worth
focusing on.
For this is what
we came here to do
and achieve
with the Help of
The Holy Spirit
and according to
God's Plan

RE Mistress of reality...
I guess we only earn the title
Master and Mistress
when we fulfill our destiny...
To know that we are in this world
but not of it
in every moment
of NOW!
That is what keeps us
from truly being Masters
of the world we made
to mock our Self!
How painful this must be
until the lesson is learned
COMPLETELY...
Then it becomes laughable.
I only know
that what we don't Laugh at NOW...
is what we still
need to learn...
So that is the agenda...and the curriculum.

Holding grievances
is an attack
on God's Plan for salvation.
Only the "when" is up to us.
So we can stay in the drama
for as long as we wish
but sooner or later
in this lifetime or next
we will take off that mask
and wake up
to the fact...
that "nothing really is happening here"
except our reactions.

Our Holy Father
We come to you tonite
Asking for YOUR Rest
We would let go of that which we have made
as a substitute for Your Creations
of Which we Are
as Your SON...One.
We lay down our dreams and illusions
and come to you with open mind
and ask for the Peace of God
which is Our Inheritance
and the Key to Our Home with YOU.
We give Thanks and Gratitude
for the Holy Spirit
who is with Us
and Who Guides Us
here tonite.
for this we say together,
Amen

ONLY our Decision
to say I don't need
to do this anymore
or I don't need
to do that again
will end the chains...
of effect, effect, effect.

The request for
Peace NOW
and REST in GOD
will carry you through
storms and strife,
past misery and pain
past loss and death...
There is no suffering
it cannot heal
since it is the
decision
to turn Our mind
to its rightful Source.
It restores
our Mind
to its Creative Power
which we Share
with Our Creator.
The Love of Creation can Cure.

We have all come
to this point in our lives
when something seems
to disturb us
and we seek
whatever means
we have available to explain
what happened
or to find solace
in talking about it.
These are just adding
more dreams to the dreams
that got us there.
The beliefs in hurt and betrayal
are the same illusions
that will continue to haunt us
until we decide
to wake up
from the dream
and see it
for what it is.

It was an opportunity
to FORGIVE
and let go.
We do know
that it was
a Lesson.
Once learned
that need not be
learned again...
or we can repeat it
if we wish.
The choice is ours.

We do need
to change our Mind.
That is the Purpose
of The Course
It is a gentle way
of beginning
to see things differently.

Everyone here
sees the Teacher
in each
and every
One here.
We are All Blessed.
Teachers are all around us.
It is for us
to See them...
so Seek.

We do meet
our unexpected Teacher
in this world
in many places.
And sometimes
it is easy to see
the Christ in them.
And sometimes
our Teacher
looks a lot like Judas.
In both cases... it is the Same.
It is our function
to Restore
the Sonship as WHOLE.
And All are given to us
to Include...
and when we finally do...
The Love that
the course
does not Teach
is US.

Creating thru Communication
with the loving eyes
of Forgiveness...
which sees His brother
in a deep sleep,
like a little child
who is in a deep dream,
knows that he is Safe
within the Mind
of God
and knows that
He will Awaken
on his own
in His own time
since he is his Brother
and a Co-Creator with God
is then shared with his own Self.
This is the message
that the Holy Spirit
give us to take
to our Brother...
wherever
we meet him
or whomever
is sent to us.
205
Close your eyes
and look within
and smile.
You will see
it...
:-)
206

The funniest thing about the word illusion
is that there is only one.
The belief in "we are separate".
That one belief
is what made this
insane world we live in.
The so-called veils
is the fear...or the blocks...
to the AWARENESS
of WHO WE ARE
AS ONE
AS LOVE.
Without Limitation.
Unconditional.
This is our Reality.
Of course
it sounds easy to say
and when we use the tools
that this world of separation
gives us
which is the sight and sounds
and thoughts...of the physical senses...
207
This "illusion" seems very real.
Yet, I know we
WILL WAKE UP
and smile
and Look back
and Laugh
at all of this
just as we do
when we look back at the people
that thought
the sun rose and set for us
and the world was flat.
Now we know
the sun doesn't rise and set

we revolve and
the world is not flat.
INEVITABLY...
we will
KNOW WE ARE ONE!
Then the illusion of separation
and all of its veils
will have
disappeared.
IN OUR KNOWING WHO WE ARE!

As I see it...
you don't have to go further
than Lesson 1.
It kinda says it all.
We just don't believe it
in its entirety.
So we go on to lesson 2
and find out
that we made it all up.
We give it all the
meaning it has for us.
That's todays lesson.
That's all folks!!!!!!!!!!!!

We Give Thanks this Evening
for the Gift we have
We Thank our Father
and Jesus
for Giving Us
this moment in time
to Remember the Truth
That God is
With US
ALWAYS
and it is this GIft
That we would
Give to our Brother
and to see this world
Through His Loving Eyes
that
ONLY EXTENDS
HIS JOY
TO US ALL
Amen

What is God's Vision...
How does God Create?
BY Joining
or JOYning
By Extending to include.
So...YES
God is in everything I see
because everything
and everyone
is part of the Plan
To bring the Sonship Home.

It is already written.
We are playing
out the part
we agreed to play
along time ago.
Yes...everything here is joined
for the
Purpose of our
Oneness.
We are asked
to see the things
and people in our lives
differently...
Above all else
let me see this differently.

Let me change
how I see
with the Power
and the Light
and Love
of God within.
And in this
new way of seeing
will I be Healed...
and the world
will be seen differently.
For it has a unified place
in God's Plan for our Salvation.

For the moment
you think of someone...
They are with you.
And What you Think,
or How you See them,
is your Relationship
with that person.
Vision
is different than seeing
with the body's eyes.
As the eyes see things
as near or far.
And distance in time
and space
are an excuse for not seeing at all.
YET WITH GOD,
The Idea of that person
in your mind
is JOYned
the moment you
think of them.

There is a Smile
in my Heart tonite Father.
It is a Smile of Strength
and Peace
and Comfort
as I now say
God is in everything I See
because God is in my Mind.
With me and my Brothers Always
and His Will which is Ours
is Joyned for the Purpose
of our Homeward Journey.
THANK GOD
Amen

If you WANT PEACE NOW
and that is
the Purpose of ACIM
Inner Peace...
NOW
We are asked
to Choose the Teacher of Peace
who does not see differences
between this and that...
him or her...etc. etc.
He Sees us
ALL THE SAME
and In His Knowing
We Are ONE...
His SON.

Tonite we come Together
and Give our Thanks
For Our Father's Blessings
For His Love Extends
and Gives Us
Life Eternal
We Give Thanks
for His Word
Which is Given Us
It is this that We Would Speak tonite
To ALL of our Brothers
who are Given US to Cherish
As His Own
For We Are So Loved
and Blessed and Saved
By Our Loving Father
Who Gives US His Kingdom
Always
Amen

IT
does start
within
Your Mind

WE GIVE THANKS
for
ALL THAT WE HAVE RECEIVED
and in turn
We CHOOSE TO GIVE
what we Receive here
to ALL THAT WE MEET
For only then
do we know
that we have received it.
And for all THIS
WE SAY
AMEN

I have been looking
at some of my own
"thoughts"
that when looked at a little deeper...
would make you laugh.
I noticed
that since I was a kid...
I have been making deals with God.
Oh...it's much better that I do this...
or it is much better that I do that
because a Higher Order will be served.
Welllllllllllll
anyone...know the word for this?
"Sacrifice".
Now every Student of the Course knows
that sacrifice
is the one thing
NOT to do.

Let us Rise Up
Awaken
and Extend Our Self
to Our Same Self.
The sacrifice we think we make
for the greater good
is not.
And whenever
we think
we are making
a bargain with God
we are making a bargain
with the ego.
WHO KNOWS US NOT.

Be Happy...

Peace NOW
not later.
The Answer
lies
in our
Willingness to recognize
that we do not know
and we do not understand
what we are seeing.

The Answer
is to ASK.
To let go
of our past thoughts
and ASK the Holy Spirit
to Show us.
To intercede
and Let Our Right
Minded Thoughts
be shown to us.
Any other act
or interpretation
keeps us within
the ego's domain.

KNOW THIS SELF>>called LOVE.

We have with us
another Voice...
that does not speak first
and is described as
the still quiet voice
that Knows
Who We Are
and is Ready as a Guide
to point the
Way to Peace...
and Home.
It is This Peace
that is the necessary ingredient
for us to
KNOW THE LOVE that is PRESENT
which is OUR SELF
Extended to the WHOLE.

The Course says...
We have a Choice
in every moment of Now
TO be Cause...
of what we see
To extend Ourself
to include
what we see.
This is True Cause and Effect

Basically...
we are always teaching
what we teach is up to us
and we would want
to Teach to our Self
what we would
Truly want to Learn.

IT SAYS...
GOD only
KNOWS HIS OWN...
FOR LIKE SEES ITSELF
or LOVE KNOWS ITSELF.
It is like a password...for HEAVEN.
ONLY LOVE ITSELF can enter.
Alien thoughts cannot.
Heaven being
THE Mind of God.

We Give
Thanks
and
Gratitude
for ALL of the Gifts
of Peace and Love
we have received
We Share this
by Extending our Love
to ALL
Amen

Let's Join Together
as ONE
as WE ARE
and See
Our Father's Love
and Truth
Which Shines and Extends
Through US ALL!
Amen

We are reminded
OF OUR FATHER
Who Created
US IN HIS PERFECT LOVE
and We as His Co-Creators
Extend
HIS WHOLE LOVE
TO ALL of OUR CREATIONS...
Except when we forgot to laugh...
and then we "thought" we could do it our self
and VOILA...
We made this world
of perception...and projection...
based on a belief system
that is totally false
yet pretty real in this world we made
of separation
and separate interests
in denial of
Our ONE Father
and HIS PERFECT LOVE...WHICH IS US.
So therefore...in denial of OUR SELF.

Whatever...
we are saying
or thinking about another,
and I do mean ANYTHING
WE ARE ALWAYS TALKING ABOUT OURSELF.
In this illusion
it only SEEMS
that we are talking about another.
You might say
there is nobody out there
BUT YOU
Wherever you look.

NEVER BE FOOLED BY FORM

I truly feel
that one of the
most valuable ideas
that can be Taught
by our Educators and Teachers
at an early age
are the basics of projection
which is probably
the real cosmic joke.
Since whatever
we ever say
is about OUR SELF.

Question...
Is everyone clear...
that when you point a finger
that there are 3 fingers
pointing back at you?????

What the ego
uses to keep separation
"alive and well"
WE CAN USE.
If used properly
to "recognize
what is still UNFORGIVEN
within ourselves
or what we have
not forgiven another for.
These are the two scenarios
that exist
within the realm
of projection
WHICH can BE CORRECTED
when FINALLY SEEN
by those that ARE WILLING.
This is what is valuable
about recognizing
our projections.

WE ARE EACH RESPONSIBLE
only for OUR OWN AWAKENING
and each of us needs to recognize
what we made
and BE RESPONSIBLE
for our unmaking...or undoing.
Which of course is in our minds.
It is seeing the dream
as a dream
interpreting it correctly
and WAKING UP
from what is not real.
And we are all doing this
TOGETHER.

As I SEE IT...
we are all BOTTLED LIGHT.
And when we choose to let go...
and Let God
The Light
SHINES
right through
that bottle.

Heaven itself
is reached
with empty hands and open minds
and SHARING with THE SONSHIP

First...
If in the "heat" of the moment
we can Remember
to Invite the HS...in...
into the Moment
we have gone from
an "insane" state...
or a dreaming or sleeping state
to a place of Awakening
to the possibility
that there is something Other
than the Dream.
And the more
we can access this place
and the faster
we can do it
without staying in the "heat" of the dream
the faster we are learning
to Heal our Mind
and to Awaken.

WE GIVE THANKS
for
WHO WE ARE
and For Who Our Creator IS!!!
For in this
TRUTH
is
ALL WE SEEK
Amen

Giving up complete control,
a letting go
requires us...
To Accept the Atonement.
And that is what
this Course is about.
Yet...as we all know...
Inevitably...
WE WILL LET GO
and TRUST...
in the Process.
We are under
His Guidance
Always...
even when
we choose
not to listen.
Thank God.....

It came to me
in a Vision.
That in this world
walking on water
is simply
rising above the world
and not sinking
underneath
into the deep sleep
of the world's dream.
ZZZZZZZZZZZZzzzzzzzzzzzzzzz

What is the Courses definition of guilt?
Wellllllllllll...
The first thing that comes to me is
the idea of blame,
shame or
wrong doing....
that which cannot be undone.
Yet, since the idea of this world is a mistake
and not "Created"...
that which happens in this world...
is of our own making.
And that which is made...
can be undone or unmade
by Remembering Our True Identity
and that of Our Brother
Which is Created by LOVE...
God.
That which is unlike LOVE...
is not real.
Does that provide any light?

The idea of our own guilt
is the double edge sword
that comes from the belief
in other's guilt
when we keep "guilt" alive
by making it real
by seeing it in others
the source of that guilt
remains with us.

IYSIYGI
If You Spot It You Got It...
You cannot see something in another...
that is not present in you.

If we get serious
about this Course...
We need to change our mind
as to what we Truly Want.
If we wholly desire something...
PEACE
It is Ours.

Yes...
whenever we experience pain
with regard to another...
Our Brother...
it reveals something within us...
that has been left "unhealed".
And our Brother
is acting as a catalyst....
or as you say...a mirror
to allow us to see
that within...
which we are blinded from...
and because of the way we are hardwired
...only see without.

The reason is clear.
We come here
and Gather
In His Name
To Heal.
To Ask for the Peaceful
way of seeing.
And because
of Our Purpose
It is Given to us.
Sooo...
It is in the coming together
that we find Our Self,
In each other.
That is the Idea of the Course.

Yes, time is not real...but we can waste it.

Even the Holy man...
who goes to the top of the mountain
to meditate
to find God
to Know God
knows that sooner or later
he must come down the mountain
into the village
and...of course...
when someone steps on his toe
whether he is wearing sandals or not
he gets to see God...
or not...
depending on
the Teacher
he has Chosen.

Our minds
are cause.
And the thoughts we think
come directly from the goals
and teacher we choose.
And we keep going in that direction
almost like a stream of water
until WE...
Change the Goal
and the TEACHER.
Only then,
can we Remember
Our Goal is
To Know Our Self
and in this world...
That means
giving
Gentle Graciousness
to your
Brother.

Let's Gather
for Prayer...
We Thank Our Self
for Giving us this
ONEderful Gift
This Course
that would speed
our Journey
Home
GODSPEED
Amen

Father,
We would remember
What you have
Given to us
Is Everything
and we would remember
to seek not
outside of Our Self
for that Is What we Seek...
You
Amen

What we cannot recognize
in this world,
while we are blinded
by the idols
and illusions we made,
our miscreations,
is the AMAZING LOVE
that WE HAVE.
An ETERNAL LOVE...
of which
we are an EXTENSION OF.
So...when we read the Course
and find out what the purpose
of these idols
we make and pursue
in trying to FILL
our scarcity...of Love,
the...only "sin"
is the mistaken belief
that we are not LOVED.
IT IS ONLY THIS KNOWLEDGE
that leads us to the Peace of God.
And it is only this Knowledge...
that is worth pursuing.
For the Truth will set us Free
is...
what IS WITHIN
...and nowhere else

Why is that person
always the perfect person for us
even though it doesn't "look like that"?
1st...Because they cannot give
us...what we think we need.
2nd...They give us another opportunity...to
RETHINK...
and ask to see it differently...
by saying...
There must be a better way.
Only in this way
can what seem like a nightmare,
which it is,
give us ONE MORE CHANCE...
to WAKE UP.
Which is the only way out...
of a dream.

When one finds one self
in a "virtual reality"
and has the willingness
to Ask.
That is the first sign of our Awakening.
As Helen Schucman said
just before the Course was given to her
"There must be a better way".
This is the mind's recognition that
what we are doing and seeing
may not be ...
the Path we wish to travel.
It is the highest thought
that the ego's
thought system
is capable of.
To look around
and Ask...
What is this for?

The Holy Spirit
sees the same.
And as His goal
is Always
Healing and Peace.
When we Ask,
we place ourself
in a place
of being Responsible
because we are.
We become Cause.
And as Cause
we can choose.
This has Power.
For we are saying
we are not at effect
of what we made.
What we made
to deceive
our self.

This world
is one
where you seek.
and do not find
for what we seek
is not here.
It is Our Self

The Course...as we know
is a highly
personalized Curriculum....
which asks us ...
simply to practice
the Lessons...
That Universal dating service...
will always serve up to you...
exactly who...
what you require...
for your Learning...and Healing
to be completed
IF WE CHOOSE TO SEE IT!
does that make sense?

...it's almost like
"Central casting"

Every time we Ask...
We are Asking
for a new beginning.
For if we don't...
We are accepting
the direction
we have been
heading in

YET...the goal
will remain the same
The recognition
Of Your Oneness.
The accepting of the Atonement.
The letting go
of the beliefs
in this world we made.
To demonstrate that
"separation is real".
Sooner or later...
will happen.
Of that ...
I am Confident.
For it is inevitable.
For as ACIM says...
the script is already written
and its end
has already happened.
For we are ONE!

The goal of the Course...
is not Knowledge.
It is PEACE.
For If we set this as our Goal...
NOW
The Knowledge will come.
Until then...
we are caught up
with the distractions
we have made.
It is this busyness
which the ego loves
that keeps us
from the
ONE THING WE WANT.
TO KNOW OUR SELF.
It is upon this Rising Up...
this Awakening...
that we recognize
the dream that we have made
to dream...
to forget...
Our Self.

I love the part of the Course
that says...
when you finally do wake up
from this illusion
this virtual reality
you will look back
at what you took
so seriously...
and thought was so real
and you will smile...
and even Laugh!

It is in doing the daily Lessons
and applying it
to whatever comes up
that any real Light
can be shed.
A lot of this
may not
seem to make sense
without a structure
which this can be seen
in a quiet place
otherwise...our subconscious
takes over
and a lot of stuff comes up
and kinda muddies the water.
The purpose of the Lessons
is to Still the mind
so that which
IS....
can Shine.

So, I am Happy...
that at this Easter time
we can Share Together
This Resurrection...
in the Light.
For as she said..."Purpose Unifies".
For Our Joined Purpose...
Is Healing...
and Awakening
so that each
may as Jesus said
have no further use...
for sacrifice
of any kind
for his...as he says...in the Text
was the last unnecessary ...sacrifice.

Yeah
that's the silliness.
of this stuff
we'd rather be right
and smart...
than Happy
CHOOSE AGAIN NOW
it's that easy
simple.
let go...
Or can we?

If
you are following
your Purpose
and fulfilling it
the universe bends
to see
that your Will
will be
done.

AHHHHHHHH
to
REST IN GOD...
a
mental moment

Close your eyes.
and
go withIN.
and you
are
CLOSE
to
KNOWING

To speak about
what I have come to understand
and learn
from ACIM in the past 21 years
I say it is simple
because the understanding for me
has been...
it seems to resonate with something
that I just know is True.
Yet ...
it has been far from easy
in actually carrying out
and practicing.
For as we all know
the way to Carnegie Hall
is practice, practice, practice.

So I can say...right up front
if there was one thing
I "wish" I had done
a long time ago
would be to practice
what the Course is here to Teach.
Simply...
to Free our minds
from what we fill it with
and spend at least 5 minutes
upon Awakening every day
and 5 minutes
before going to sleep every night
With Our Father
and His Spirit...with US.
For that would make
all the difference in the world.
I assure YOU
that this is the secret
to Awakening.
I see the Course
as a Self Awakening...reSource.
For that is the Purpose
to Awaken
from the sleep
which we put ourselves in.
and this is the crux of the Course.

We are given
the world's thought system
when we enter it.
It teaches
differences and specialness...
And we can
Choose God's Curriculum...
And if we do
the choices we made
and make in this world
seem silly
and a waste
of time

Yes...
You can hold onto the past
and try to understand
NOW
from our teachings of the past.
Or we can start
from scratch
NOW...
and ASK for God's Curriculum
to Fill our Mind.
The rest of it
is just busyness
for the mind
to keep you distracted
from
OUR SELF
which INCLUDES
ALL...in the Kingdom.

What you
dwell on...
expands
in your mind...

Love...
doesn't acknowledge
any of this stuff...
different world
...'tis true
our feelings
get bruised so easily
hurt seems so real
slights are obtrusive attacks
to this insanE...
God Sends His Teachers
who of course
have to release their own
demons
FIRST.

We are all familiar
with the Course term,
I Need do nothing.
Though this term is a Fact,
and it is so
for most of us,
As we move from
our sleep of dreams
and thoughts
that this world teaches us
it may be said
slightly differently...
I don't need
do that again...
and
I don't need
do that
anymore.

To Rest
is certainly
not the same word
that this world
has come to define it as...
To rest
is to
not continue
the long chain
of dreams
that only breed
more dreams

I Rest in God...
is like turning
the navigation
over to the
Automatic Pilot
Who is given
to you
that knows
the Course.

To Have Faith
in One
that is With
you
for only then
will you know
that
He
is.

We are Grateful
for the Rest
you Give US
when we Ask for it
Truly
You have given Us
your Peace and Love
tonite
and we feel
your Strength and Light
within
Let us remember
How easy
it is to
Be Here
for it is
Your Will
and Ours
that We do This
in Your Name
Amen

The Mind
that embraces
Its Creator...Love Itself
can see
His Light IN all we meet.
The projections
we place on our brother
are turned over to
The Holy Spirits' Sight
And we ask to see
our Brother in that Light.
That we are
the Love of God
Created to
Extend that Love.
That is the choice
we have every friday...
to make friday...
SONDAY.

GODSPEED

There is a lesson there too.
"God is in everything I see...
because God is in my MIND".
So see it differently
and know that
the Purpose
is part of the PLAN.
Only the ego...
wants to stand
on its head
since it
doesn't know
which side
is up
anyway.

There is a Purpose to this
When seen correctly...
you can see it
and know that
no real harm
is being done.
We all receive lessons.
Some younger
than others
it doesn't matter
it is all within
the PLAN.
already.

When seen
correctly...
the lesson
only confirms
that all is
OK
and you are asked
only to
TRUST
when not seen correctly
a lesson
can be learned
but not always.

Then I turned the page
and there was lesson 30.
and it made A LOT OF SENSE.
This reverses the worlds thinking.
God is not
out there
somewhere
that you meet
after going through all of the hoops
and passing all of the tests
and learning all your lessons.
I looked into the reflection
of the SON
and it was
SO BRIGHT
and it was like GOD
looking thru my eyes
to see my Brother
I always had a thing between Sun and Son.

Well...
If the lesson attracted you
it must be one
that you could
Share
from your Heart.
And that is where the Beauty is.
ohhhhh david

two lights in the night
shine so much brighter
together...
and within
each other
they
GLOW

YOU JUST LOVE
YOURSELF
A LOT MORE
AROUND ME
and
I LOVE MYSELF
A LOT MORE
AROUND YOU
that is how
LOVE works
IT'S CONTAGIOUS

This peace and quiet,
so wonderful tonight
'tis the Door to Heaven
PEACE
It is the
PEACE
that lets you know
what heaven
is..........
yes... :-)
And those you find it with
are gifts
you give to your Self
all that you share
see you in the GLOW
so sit close

We are
TOTALITY
and
ETERNALLY ONE.
For Our
LIGHT GOES ON FOREVER
stay there...

A
SHARED LOVE
whose
LIGHT
IS SO BRIGHT
that nothing
of this world
can even imagine
its
GLORY

Your Mind
is
certainly
ONE...
with
my Mind.

So our function
which is to bring
PEACE
and Extend it
starts simply
by letting go
of what the world is doing
and be the Radiator
of
LIGHT and PEACE
which is Extended
to us.
In this way
we are fulfilling
the reason for which
we came here

I truly believe
that
we are Teaching
that part of Our Self
that will take these Thoughts
and help to build the Bridge
from where we were
when we were born into this world
to the opposite...shore
which is within US.
This is the opposite of everything
this world teaches.
and it is WHAT ACIM does Teach.

The beliefs
in hurt and betrayal
are the same illusions
that will
continue to
haunt us
until we decide
to wake up
from the dream
and see it
for what it is.

Only that
Which is already corrupt
can rust
That which is WHOLE
remains perfect
Let it GO
can't hold something together
if it will leave
anyway.

We know
LOVE
when we Hear it
because
it brings us to
a Peaceful Place
301
The Call
to us touches us
in a
very deep and Holy Place
and
the Call...
is stronger
than the call
of the world.

Every step was a stepping stone
that prepared my mind
for understanding
what the Course was saying
so that when it came
I embraced it.

And it certainly
RESONATES
with
everything I know
and
feel.

THANKS for Listening
to myself
Teach My Self

Let us Gather
and
Remember
We are One
In Our
ONENESS
nothing is lost.
Herein Lies the
Peace of God
Amen

Laughter now...
Saves Lifetimes
Later
307
Love and Peace Always,
David

and now
back
to the dream

231, 243–244, 252, 255,
259, 263, 273–274, 277–
279, 288, 294, 296–297,
301, 315

About the Author

David Fishman has been a leading teacher of A Course In Miracles for over 30 years. He has used its principles of spiritual psychology as a basis or relationship counseling. David is the author of Into Oneness, Thoughts & Prayers on the Way and is currently working on his next book.

He moderates A Course In Miracles meetings on the Internet and maintains a website at www.ACIMgather.org. Since 1998. David was the Chair of the Human Rights Commission of Yonkers as well as serving as Commissioner.

Co-Founder of ONEMIND Foundation Sponsor of ACIM Gather, a worldwide portal for developing trust in our True Self. And Open Minds for ACIM & NTI, a forum for its members to share their Blessings.

Colophon

Titles: Myriad Pro
Text: Minion Pro

Set in Adobe Indesign 5.5
Printed in USA
Designed by Spirit Press

www.onespiritpress.com
onespiritpress@gmail.com

Made in the USA
Middletown, DE
15 July 2017